Tocqueville

Khaled Mattawa

New Issues Poetry & Prose

A Green Rose Book

New Issues Poetry & Prose
The College of Arts and Sciences
Western Michigan University
Kalamazoo, Michigan 49008

First Edition, 2010.

ISBN-10:   1-930974-90-6 (paperbound)
ISBN-13:   978-1-930974-90-6 (paperbound)

Library of Congress Cataloging-in-Publication Data:
Mattawa, Khaled
Tocqueville/Khaled Mattawa
Library of Congress Control Number: 2009939909

Art Direction: Barbara Loveland
Design: Josh Tabbia
Production: Paul Sizer
                 The Design Center, Frostic School of Art
                 College of Fine Arts
                 Western Michigan University
Printing: McNaughton & Gunn, Inc.

Tocqueville

Khaled Mattawa

New Issues

WESTERN MICHIGAN UNIVERSITY

Tocqueville

Also by Khaled Mattawa

Amorisco
Zodiac of Echoes
Ismailia Eclipse

For Gretchen, Iman, and Chase;
and for Fouad

Contents

Lyric

Will answers be found
like seeds
planted among rows of song?

Will mouths recognize
the hunger
in their voices, all mouths in unison,

the ah in harmony, the way words
of hope are more
than truth when whispered?

Will we turn to each other and ask,
how long
has it been . . . how long since?

A world now, a world then
and each
is seeking a foothold, trying

to remember when we looked
at one another
and found—A world again— Surely

what we long for is at the wheel
contending.

Surely, we'll soon hear
its unearthly groan.

On the Difficulty of Documentation

The village women carry the moon on their heads.

Each carrying a piece.

Or each carrying her own moon,
the jugs of white stoneware in Myrtle Winter's photo.

See how light spills into their dark robes—

> In thin array after a pleasant guise,
> When her loose gown from her shoulders did fall. (Wyatt)

Its white deluge is the phosphorescence of their headscarves radiating
   against twilight.
Each a planet then, rejoining a galaxy on the run.

I recall: Such people have no time for beauty.

I recall: Beauty is one of the great conversation stoppers of all time.

Evidence is plentiful that the twilight these women walk is a betrayal:
The child whose skin is a crumbled sack around the muscles of his
   legs and buttocks.

Look at how his mother's beauty is fleeing.

Look at the faces that evoke an age-old deferral:

> Alas, we
>   who wished to lay the
>   foundations of kindness
> could not ourselves be kind.

> But you, when at last it
>   comes to pass . . .

> do not judge us too harshly. (Brecht)

Do not judge us for this strange fashion of forsaking (Wyatt) because
   what beauty does is almost a crime (Brecht)

and what the photographer's eyes take from them must be a kind of
     theft too—

    But why do
               they flee from me
       these beauties
               that sometime did me seek (Wyatt)

into refugee tents, weighed down with thirst

toward children whose shaved heads gleam and men whose faces are
     horoscopes of dejection?

And what of that look, and the all too human?

To be enthralled

    and fain know what she hath deserved (Wyatt)

    the squalor that makes the brow grow stern
    the just anger that turns a voice harsh. (Brecht)

What else could she do, as she parts, but softly say,

    Oh dear heart, how like you this? (Wyatt)

And I recall how

    They flee from me, gentle, tame and meek
         how they range
    Busily seeking with continuous change. (Wyatt)

Bread & Butter

What lies beyond sorrow belongs to feet, automobiles, and the distances they cover. When leaves change color, no one will say, "True, true, again." Yes, steps in an endless ladder, conjectures about the size of infinity, deviations from the arrangements of our best composers. Ask sopranos about this; they will tell you all there is to know.

I begin with warm ground under my feet. It's the old argument about progress, how today's bakers deprive us of the dialectics of tooth and grain, earth and tongue, so that in kneading only the palm is happy meeting one of its own. Sometimes these encounters end up in the food chain, the body hording them for its endless famines.

There is no escaping the white rose, the wish for shade on hot summer days. But will longing explain the mystique of dying words? And before imagining the possibility of redemption shouldn't we consider why gravediggers refuse to dig alone? Some of us die before asking questions. Some of us consult witch doctors who decipher the lines on zebras' backs.

We turn to bakers and ask, what do they deprive themselves of. At home they comment on the rice, the grilled meat or beans. No mention of bread. You say this is the stamp of distance, or that we live by the apotheosis of pleasures and sufferings. Then you and I share a dream of drowning. And though we want to be saved, we hope it is the bakers who sail past us on a raft.

Can anything, other than birds, provide a better answer? A man with many keys is trustworthy. Yet locksmiths are regularly tested by the authorities. Divorces deny them access to safes. A glass of wine limits their clientele to people locked out of their cars. And that's when the keyless realize the freedom self-effacement grants. In the vast parking lots of November they begin to reflect on melting and solidifying, and on the whisper of salt in their morning butter. Look at how they stand lonely and content.

Ecclesiastes

The trick is that you're willing to help them.
The rule is to sound like you're doing them a favor.

The rule is to create a commission system.
The trick is to get their number.

The trick is to make it personal:
No one in the world suffers like you.

The trick is that you're providing a service.
The rule is to keep the conversation going.

The rule is their parents were foolish,
their children are greedy or insane.

The rule is to make them feel they've come too late.
The trick is that you're willing to make exceptions.

The rule is to assume their parents abused them.
The trick is to sound like the one teacher they loved.

And when they say "too much,"
give them a plan.

And when they say "anger" or "rage" or "love,"
say "give me an example."

The rule is everyone is a gypsy now.
Everyone is searching for his tribe.

The rule is you don't care if they ever find it.
The trick is that they feel they can.

Power Point I

(January-May 2003)

What is disclosed lies smoldering
in stackings one beside the other.
Never connect, remain in a state beyond privilege
for that is why the swimmer can pursue
such unlikely heroism, and when tragedy strikes
something scoots over. A realignment
in the food chain of sympathy, all laid out,
a horizon no further than bullet range.
That's what the swimmer sees
in 32-degree water, chunks of ice bump into
her head, the crew worried gesticulating.
Penguins zooming below her like torpedoes.

A change of clothes now—the warmth of the engine
room, even in Arctic weather,
an awakening, the flesh revealing its layers—the cold
a message sent out, victory's radiance absorbed.

A change of clothes again. DAYLIGHT
EXTERIOR SHOT, merchants selling tomatoes,
equatorial sun, old colonial building. FLASHBACK TO dream
image of something monstrous, a jellyfish/dragon
pink hued green, bone breaker, blood sucker, leaves
corpses behind like mummies . . . Kampala, Nov. 13, 2:11 p.m.,
the Ugandan scientist heads out for lunch and nap.
As to the new vaccine—"Issues of equity in clinical research
preoccupy ethicists and public health officials."
But need for human subjects persists:
Email a team of programmers in Bangalore:
reams of actuarial spread sheets,
cost assessment charts, patent infringement,
distribution of affected populations, national origin
divided by the square root of race.

FLASHBACK TO Black woman dancing with her German shepherd
in post-industrial living room.

CUT TO

a house with an American flag at half mast.

Tragedy in Palestine,

Texas.

CUT TO

Arabic text of Yasser Arafat's letter of condolence
to White House.

The German shepherd is blasé about the whole ordeal.

FLASHBACK

TO 19th century church in Norwich
the minister delivering the sermon, January, steam
rises from minister's mouth.
Front row dignitaries are seated with their dogs on their feet as foot
warmers.
Minister shouts out the story of Ezekiel, and at the mention of the
wheel
the dogs bolt out.

There's of course a case to be made for war:
But the empire is circumspect.
It does not like to do things for one purpose:

Desire	Pros	Cons
Fire	Practicality	Greed
Danger	Protectiveness	Delusiveness
Interlocutor	Acumen	Mischief

SOLUTION:
Move to next point,
when that shows fizzle-effect, move on, repeat.
Return to first point.
Keep adding additional nuances.
Let them think you're practical, greedy, protective of citizens, trigger-
happy, sissy, inconsistent, hypocrite all at the same time.

Added together, averaged out
people will think you're okay.

Yes, the need for lyric persists, for to love one person
you must contemplate loving the whole world.
Some loves are demarcations of boundaries,
fears we wish to be contained within: a man who cooks
or does laundry, a woman trading at the market,
a policeman on patrol, a field being tilled, a horizon.
Herein lies the lyric moment. A particularity that fences us.
And herein the obsession with death,
childhood, illness (of a certain kind),
something to expend one's life into and or toward.
And so how can you talk to a man whose wife had died of cancer
about anything when all the pain he's capable of
has been already allotted and spent?

In the house where the Black woman is dancing with her dog, the
    dog is showing slight discipline problems;
she consults guide book:
The paw on the knee, the staring down, the leaning,
all these are gestures designed to convey higher status in clan or
    household.
Dog owner, if such behavior is demonstrated, must force dog to
    submission.

> Never give dog anything for free.
> Before you feed dog, make it sit,
> before you pet it, make it sit,
> before dog gets to go out, make it sit.

Sometimes with an undisciplined dog you will have to topple it over
and prevent it from getting up, even if that requires sitting on it, for
a minimum of five minutes, twice a day. If dog fails to respond to a
command, owner must roll dog onto its side and stare it in the eye
for fifteen seconds.

PAN SHOT (across the street)
Two men in their sixties, one blind,
talking about a shade of color, having a moderately expensive wine,
engaged in the airy metaphysics that strikes citizens
of a certain achievement confirmed
by a certain unintrusive sociopolitical confidence.

There's an underwriting notice airing
on the classical radio station to which they're not listening.
This hour is brought to you by
     134 colonial adventures
     slavery
     depletion of fresh water, lumber, oil, and coal.

Everything meanwhile is coated with a substance as fine as Anthrax.
Even the swimmer who's grown her hair long so
that she'd pile it on her head like a turban for better insulation,
her face too is speckled with the dandruff of conquest.

Time now to ask the Nobel prize winner, "If the swimmer died, would
she be a martyr?" "A martyr dies unwillingly," he says. Someone has
an important follow-up question, something about the fighters who
died defending the Warsaw ghetto, and other possible places like it,
but the questioner does not ask his question because it's improper to
make such comparisons.

On her second try the swimmer went farther because she could not
feel pain. Yesterday's swim killed some of her nerve endings. Cold
blood from the extremities disrupts the heart's normal processes.
There are potential applications for this concept in the real world, but
why take the dark turn, why mistake the swimmer's head-gear for
that of the one-eyed mullah of Kandahar?

Why do so when there's a tide pulling at the mind's bearings?
It rises and at its peak nerve endings stand like nettles,
the soul's wheels spinning like a grinding mechanism,
the eyes are coated by previous visions that become the future.

     Where are you off to my love/
     on this cold rainy day/
     The birds you hear singing/
     are not on this land/
     The rays that warm your arms/
     and cheeks are not shining/
     from the sun/

Where are you off to my love/
on this cold rainy day/
The dry firm earth you walk/
is no earth at all/

Hence, no way to shut down the Sapphic pipeline. Traces of it were
found near Baku by
Caltex geologists, and in the blue eyes of the late mujahideen leader
Massoud Shah.

The movie had commercials for The Gap, Kawasaki, Citibank, etc,
embedded in it. The film's main dilemma is whether the hero should
kill or not kill.

Nothing is likely to happen in the present when we believe the
moment lived has already slipped out into an unrecoverable past, a
past through which all events have been framed. Otherwise it's the
future we must look forward to, and it's horrifying; it's moving at a
G force beyond our familiar disappointments. That's why the hero of
the movie will need to acquire magical powers or the latest technology.
This is the place where the hero resides, where he must choose
between killing or not killing.

The dog owner opens a magazine and reads about the swimmer's
accomplishment
which is to have become for a short while the cogwheel driving the
second-arm of civilization's time,
because to say Empire is to say: the Tet offensive and one step for
man,
and going out to the movies and making sure the dog does not maul
the new sofa,
wherein the blind man's accomplishment, via an eye bank in
Bombay, is another toddle unto revelation,
so many magical powers or advanced technology incorporated
within
where the march of progress becomes loops and loops of human
matter strung around the cinemaplex,

the human soul as a conglomerate, a spark plug winking within the
        universe's internal combustion,
triumphs like motes of pollen from new epochs stinging the
        Cyclops's eye,
so much dithering, a catharsis that hurls us screaming unto the street,
        our faces coated with history.

Later, Later

Both here and in other traces, footprints and droppings, cobwebs and the blackened stones that bank all fires. Someone will resist, and words will scatter like the beads of a rosary suddenly breaking.

The scene is afternoon, my favorite time of day, a dentelle veil, an underbelly of light, darkness lurking in ovens sharpening claws.

What will my mother say? Sunflowers in the fields. To watch them is to ask for dizziness by its other name.

Time ticks on the wall, on your wrist bones. It flashes mercurial on the empty roads of the Middle West. Someone will resist and a new song will nest in our heads and a river will run between hands as they shake a doubtable peace.

A long time ago I hid in a bean field. A long time ago a story waited for its evil twin. Worms glistening in sunlight. Mud on my knees and red mud and a life spent panning the stream bed. The shrapnel of a life—ligaments and filaments—a gun fight, a piano, ragtime bubbling from the fingers of a whiskered man. She lights a cigarette. She is a young sought-after prostitute. But I did not know that till later, till I saw one, a fifty-year-old Maltese.

Later, later. I told him to pick up my bag when I run. I punch him in the face and run. You understand?

The preacher coughed bitterly. Is he dying, I ask.

It happened in London and the story waited for its merchant husband to return. She was old and naked and smoked a cigarette and said you have a chipped tooth and you are young. You must be terrible in bed.

How did it happen? I told you wait. Pick up my bag and run. How did it happen? I waited in the mud in my favorite time of day and I knew someone would resist. Was it me? Someone will look if such things are to be found.

You idiot, I said.

All of this happened later.

It all began with mud, said the preacher I loved. It all began with mud, and coughed.

Airporter

Yardley, Pennsylvania, an expensive dump
and the van seats shake their broken bones.

Duty-free liquor and cigarettes,
the refineries and the harbor's cranes.

The moon digs its way out of the dirt.
The branches of an evergreen sway.

She's nice
the woman you don't love.

She kisses you hard and often
holding your face in her big hands.

Terrorist

Reading night and the fire that lances
the sky, reading day and the arabesques
of strewn corpses, I become my brother's
Siamese twin. Rubbing the ashes of his
bones unto my face I become his blue
screams at birth. And despite what I've
told myself, what I've grown to believe,
despite my bunkered heart and fortified
skin, my thick bile and phlegm, I am bled
white by an appalling battle. I have cleansed
my body with the soap of his fat, stuffed
my pillows with his shorn hair, I made
dice of his molars. Everything, and my
contradictions above all, bring us closer.
Will I walk on four now to recall what I
thought was human? Will I climb the tree
shedding skin, whispering the apple's secret?
What poisons will house themselves in
my gills? Will I be a victim again? And again
a murderer? I split in two and two more,
and I fill a room growing like yeast into
all the selves I've known. Everything
leads me back, unified and cellular, to
the womb we shared. Reading thunder
made in preachers' salons, reading lightening
that severs the sun's rays, my silences spill
an ooze that fastens me to him; My cowardices
hook us into one destiny. See how short
my arms are. Take a look into my blind eyes.
Every breath I inhale is the cold wind
that makes us embrace like statues of
eternal lovers. In every exhale there's a
wisp of silver smoke from the warm clay
that binds us. Reading night, reading
day, I twin myself to my brother.

Power Point II

(November 2005-February 2006)

. . . it rolls without consequence
                    rolls
demands four male witnesses
to reach judgment   one leviathan
shielding you from another.

Why not rank such acts a kind of weather?

Why not blame it on the mean old
woman
          driving down the street willing
to wipe you off the blacklist of suspects
or the father, the proverbial father
who loved his machine
             more than his inheritors.

Eight women witnesses will do because
                lyric resolution
demands an arrival into what does not suffice.
That's why the assassin has videotaped
the victim pleading for mercy, the dark cave
viewed through infra red   the reams and reams
of duct tape that bind her to a chair,
the glowing eyes of the rats as they feed:

          Who them/
          people ask me/
          all the things?/
          What appetite/
          what tools/
          and turns?/
          Translate, say/
          the red one/
          and the brown/
          wring my word/
          He pick up/
          cell phone/
          I hear word/
          for love/

I hear for cunt/
turns another/
switch/
the needles that's/
pierce my ears/
etch word/
on very very/
white screen/

The other inquisitor too wants the purity
of bones, the gleaming phosphorescence
of the cave, while the medieval psychopath
beneath his black hood, body hair shaved,
approaches the hostage's throat . . .
It is enough to turn a reporter into a novelist,
and the novelist toward myth for rescue
and the poet running toward the white heat of his soul
fed on the fuel of indignation
emitting cum-light of self-love,
a technique now perfected and taught
at military academies, a dirge played
in the pilot's head as he mans four drones
shadowing a Mitsubishi sedan driven at dawn
through the potholed streets of Nineveh.

There is no poverty of imagination   deferral
an endless soap opera   enacted multitudinously.
The commander-in-chief orders the demolition
but the need to redeem wipes out
the primordial call to split the child in half.
Luckily, these crises only occur in the middle
of the episode   leaving time for narrative
to tuck the victims into the clay of tragedy even as
the highways gridlock, the voters moving inland
                                escaping the storm.

It's not surprising then that the famous terrorist/
religious leader also has to bribe his children
to memorize the holy book, a horse for the teenage
boy to memorize the chapter of the heifer.
He too knows the citizenry does not like a complex lie,
the screen rendering a pattern of tiny
orange dots spreading on pristine Slavic snow.

William Faulkner Sartoris, I see/
your great granddaughter/
eating enchiladas/
made for her by her/
Guatemalan husband and/
they taste good to/
her, they taste good to her/
but must we wait/
for those discrepancies/
to blend/
and what gradations/
to emerge when she, your/
great great granddaughter/
already lives neither in/
Mississippi nor in Nebraska/
or anywhere not even/
in the mind . . . /

. . . CUT TO
surveillance video of
we'rewatchingyou dot org,
started by a foreign funded NGO with offices
across the street from the American university
not far from Starbucks and Plimpi,
but the activists prefer local coffee, made by a janitor
who takes courses at Alliance Française,
a law degree at Open University (in progress).
The outcome is that the head of state
in power for 24 years announces a 17-point plan.

Though the statistics say otherwise,
the compass needle continues shivering

and the disquiet goes on glowing with guilt
in rented apartments, divorced by now,
the children taking their college funds with them,
the slow slog to the laptop to update the résumé,
and it is the psychopath that wins the lottery, the ticket
printed on a Mohican's scalp.

When will this thing . . . How long . . .
asks the comedian-politician,
but even the self-made mad genius, part scientist, part Frankenstein
demurs because the answer is always too large for the question
         . . . the answer-paralysis
         demands living with the sound
         of a sound being erased.

                 . . . He opens
the windows to her house, lets in some light and air,
turns her over to undress her.
She's now a leviathan whose comical marauding forms an invisible
         fence
on the imagination, to tell us to stay here,
leading the neglectful father to join the neighborhood watch,
to meet old acquaintances, a round of golf,
returning home to powder under her sagged chest,
to rub some cortisone cream on sores between her thighs,
while she says, yes, yes, here, here, yes.

Tocqueville

An offer to discuss.
He wears a thin graying beard, kaffiyeh flaunted on shoulders.
She's got a school-marmish face, this time black.

On the Horn of Africa, pirates on the water,
technicals with Kalashnikovs on pick-up trucks,
streetlights ripped for scrap metal.
Rebel-leader president, cell phones shuddering, bank accounts in Dubai.

We are all Christians now, said Mandelstam.

/ /

Ajami, Abizeid, Rice, Gonzalez, Yoo, Viet Dinh

with people like that leading the action, you can't call it racism.

That's what you call the karma of yellow/brown folks.

/ /

If you want these people to play your national anthem
when your envoy visits,
if you want them to open a branch of the chamber of commerce,
or Chase Manhattan,
you've got set the whole thing up.
They're not going for that anymore.
And anyhow, do you know how many countries
make their own AK47's now?

And Uzi's too, but that's more of a fashion statement.

And you'd have to wonder what they're doing for water and electricity.

Everybody's got generators now. Some people installed windmills on
        their roofs,
Chinese made, Danish technology. Kerosene less expensive than water.

And hasn't everybody's dug a well and a pump to suck whatever municipality water gets through the old pipes?

What municipality water? That's all gone now. The sewage system
          has been out for years.

You could make good money building cisterns there, and good money renting the trucks that suck the shit out.

You dump it in the sea, of course.

/ /

"From Aristotle on, republican theorists have stressed the importance of the middle class for the success of free institutions. Neither powerful nor powerless they vacillate between a desire to protect what they possess and the freedom to acquire more. They split the difference by deifying the liberty granted to each of them. They agree to disagree, the bonds formed between them are the daggers they have thrust into each other's backs. They see this as an ideal kind of harmony, and they are willing to die for it. Which is why images of the demonstrators singing a hymn or being beaten by the police is discombobulating. The scent of virtue begins to sting your eyes because you know it's rising from a pile of burning corpses."

I like it, but do you think anyone but a leftist or fascist review would publish it?

/ /

Sometimes I want to call what I see
through the keyhole "a flower."
Then I see the clock racing,
the digits tumbling over themselves.

Then I turn to her face
and ask a question of love.

// /

"An orderly, gentle, peaceful slavery which could be combined more
easily than is generally supposed, with some of the external forms of
freedom and there is a possibility of getting itself established even
under the shadow of the sovereignty of the people."

/ /

You just have to look at her face and wonder.
Could she have been best friends with one of the little girls from
Alabama?

You almost said, "long ago"

And then you see the way he raised his arms as if he's pleading, or
like one of the singers from that world, and you know she'll never
understand him. She'll say, "we're not talking to you," and she'll
sound just like putting her teenage girl under curfew. That stern face.
Then she'll send an envoy.

Does she have a teenage daughter?

I don't know, but I hear she's dating a Canadian diplomat.

The Canadian foreign minister, and he looks like a young Max Van
Sydow.

Who's that?

A Swedish actor, he plays Nazi officers all the time, very blonde.

So what do you make of that?

It's called the Electra complex.

//

All the nightclubs in the city have closed. They have become refugee camps. We sing at wedding parties, maybe once a month. If we had a concert, the militias might come and rob the audience, and us, but they would make sure they enjoyed the music first. The wedding parties are big, spectacular affairs; you wouldn't think they were in a country without a government. Only the people from the big, armed clans can have these parties. Other people just get married in secret.

//

He was my friend and they arrested him for uploading child pornography. He was my best friend. I didn't know how to use the internet back then, and remember him so kind, though a part of me was repulsed by his fingers, all those hand-rolled cigarettes. His father used to walk around with an oxygen tank. Had emphysema and smoked on the sly until he died. Their house was large, in a rich neighborhood, but filthy. Where did he find the babies, the toddlers? Who'd let him near them? They're almost adults now, those babies, already masturbating, fantasizing . . . The horror of it is unbearable. He was my best friend.

You sound like you loved him. Did you love him?

I must have loved him or something . . . and I feel betrayed.

Betrayed or angry?

Not angry at him, but almost at myself. I know people go wrong somewhere, but where did I go wrong with him? How come this happened to someone I cared for?

//

The first dictator said, "you mean you guys knew Marx was a Jew and never told me? We would have never adopted scientific socialism had I known." And now with binoculars from his capital's port, he could practically see Jeddah, and dream away.

Now, that was long ago.

Yeah, I was the one who sent him the binoculars, through the Kuwaiti ambassador.

/ /

My shrink called at the time of the appointment. He didn't want to be technical, but said you canceled in less than 24 hours. I didn't want to technical either, but I told him that I canceled within 23 and a half hours. Still, I don't blame him. If time is not money, what is it? And in that hour he was supposed to make money, what was he going to do with himself? In the small office, I could hear other patients talking with the therapist next door. Many times I tried to overhear what the other people were saying. I'd put down my head as if I'm thinking about what I'm trying to say, but I was just listening to what was being said next door. In the waiting room there weren't enough magazines, so the patients didn't know what to do. I know we never want to see each other again, not in the clinic, not in the supermarket, not anywhere. A few minutes to the hour, the shrinks come out calling our names, each taking a patient to his office. There must have been twenty offices inside. Not tastefully decorated, something between Super Eight and Red Roof Inn. Always a box of kleenex near where the patient sat. I remember during one visit when I reached for the tissues and cried. It felt good to cry, I'm not a crying-type of person, but when you overhear other people crying across the walls, and you walk out after the session and you'd been crying and you see someone else who'd been crying you just wonder what's happening here.

//

Ever tried to pinpoint yourself in one,
how they shimmer like nocturnal cityscapes viewed from the sea.

Or the way the satellite eye zooms down
on your house, and then out and out (like in the movies).

A scent grows in the mind then:

>The fustiness, the ancient beard,
>the house made from sun-baked bricks
>and its salted sheepskins . . .
>the breath of dried palm fronds in my grandfather's house.

//

Inside the television, we see him shrinking, inside himself, shrinking.
He feels his own exhaust. He smells the no-one he has become to us.
I can't even hate him any more. That's how personal these things
can get.

So we're part of it, this place, if we can react this strongly to things
happening here.

We can't dismiss him, or them, because his actions have
reverberations everywhere.

But you're not worried about everywhere are you? Only where you
come from.

Maybe if I were from some place where what happens here has little
or no effect, I'd love being here, and I'd have other concerns.

You'd be one of us.

Something like that.

//

It just doesn't look like racism. What do you call it then?

A kind of mould, software, bedrock. You can make all sorts of people buy into it. Blacks, Hispanics, Jews, Asiatics, Arabs, Indians. That's what happens to them when they're on your side. There's already fear that makes all kinds of violence legitimate, or a desire to kill that rationalizes itself as fear of violence. In the end, it doesn't matter which. And then you take that energy outward, and like a searchlight you beam it on whatever target you want. You put black face on the target, but people, even Black people don't see what you've done. And you tell them that's the enemy, that's who's planning to kill or rape your children, and they'll shoot at it. At first out of fear, then out of the pleasure of shooting at it. That's what happened to us.

//

I have been living here at the former headquarters of the national airlines for 9 years. About 800 other families live in this building, or in the grounds. I am not working at the moment. I am 24 and I have four children.

//

Her head sideways on my arm,
she's about to fall asleep.
My face is so close to hers that my breath
makes her hair ripple like a liquid.

When I begin to kiss her face,
I don't know if I am telling her

that I can't live without her or
telling her goodbye.

Her head doesn't move;
she knows I'm wavering
and doesn't want to tip me
to one side or the other.

/ /

They found me in the house with my baby child. They'd already
killed my wife in the field. They told me to place the child in the
mortar we used to mash cassava. Then they handed me the club
and told me to bludgeon my child, or they would kill me. And I
did as they said. Afterwards, they cut off both my arms and let me
go.

/ /

"To many of us educated to believe in classical and liberal and
Western democratic values, he exemplified those values almost to
the letter. Having written his assessment of democracy in America
and having criticized American mistreatment of Indians and black
slaves, he later had to deal with French colonial policies in Algeria
during the late 1830s and 1840s. The French army of occupation
undertook a savage war of pacification against the Algerians. All
of a sudden, as one reads him, the very norms with which he had
humanely demurred at American malfeasance are suspended for
French action. Massacres leave him unmoved. The natives belong
to an inferior religion, and must be disciplined. In short, the
apparent universalism of his language for America is denied,
willfully denied to his own country, even as his country pursues
similarly inhumane policies."

Of course, I thought the whole world would change by either decision, that was what my world came to be, that moment. I had no other life, and no other event or thought could stop me from planting those kisses on her.

Did that bring you closer, the physical intimacy?

I guess so. I kept kissing her until she and I fell asleep.

Did you feel safe together, that you had something that was special to the two of you alone?

I don't know what to call it, love or exhaustion, or love by exhaustion.

Did you feel you wanted to be anywhere else?

I couldn't think of anywhere else. I felt that I was here, or there, with her. That's all.

/ /

Have you ever seen a picture of her with her husband or children? Is she married with children? Does she have a partner, and they can't afford to show that for political purposes? Ever seen a picture of her with her mom?

No, but of course this kind of context would be useful, to show a human side, the family side.

Still, it's essential that these people, that they appear alone.

Yes.

Too many of them with Yale accents now.

That's when the best form of flattery becomes menace.

They just don't want to see dark people in groups.

Yes, except in these wide-angle shots of the poor jostling and stretching out their empty bowls, I have heard you say that before. But who's they?

They is all of us.

//

I made my way through the border and into a refugee camp. Now they want us out of this country and back to our own. I will not return. What I fear is that I will meet the men who made me kill my child. I am afraid of the shame I will feel when I face them.

//

They don't have a language. They're all body.

There's twirling, cheerleading, tom toms. "Is good money here," I heard this Russian coach say. Opened up a gym in Houston to train cheerleaders, her gold medal in gymnastics inside a big cube of clear acrylic on her desk.

Those girls get up at six to jog. They lift weights, Pilates. They're nuts about the body.

Their hymens rupture from doing the split so often, I hear.

Yeah, but only you people would think that's a big deal. Wouldn't you agree with me there?

I agree. We're nuts about the hymen.

Are you worried about your daughters? Is that what this is all about?

I'm worried about my son too. That he'd become some kind of Abezeid or Veit Dinh or Yoo.

He'd have to decide that for himself.

I'd rather he become a suicide bomber than become that.

/ /

Fiber optic lines sabotaged,
the nation's eyes go astigmatic.
The movie, as we all know, is a national-emergency-drill.

/ /

Dear C:

The way a mosquito is, the way a fly is, the way a bird nests, how there is always the sweaty skin from which to draw blood, the rot to place your eggs in, the nest built with twig and wire and pillow stuffing. Call it tether, call it the sight of snow falling on the backyard's lawn. It's two, wife at work, children at school and you want to finish a chapter before your solitude is disrupted. Snow is falling, and though things will change, and though snowfall is a change in itself, what you feel is the measure of the spider web of your life, how finely crafted it is, how firm, and how it bespeaks a culture. The snowfall makes the moment resonate with times lived and experienced, and you are made denser by the mood it brings, ready to forgive everything including your own death. Images of your grown children flash before you, their graduations, marriages, births of their children, even divorces, even accidents and tragedies. You know you'll live to see it all. And it'll feel like a part of your life, but also a part of a larger life. And that just fills you with glee, how your life and expectations are coming together. I think that's what we all come to call happiness. And though you know you'll die, this twining gives you a sense of purpose, even a sense of your immortality. Your head is buzzing with revelation now, you understand what the author of the book you'd been reading had tried to say more than he understood it himself. You take down notes with immense concentration, detailing your advances upon his argument. You decide you'll make dinner, you have it all planned. Snow is falling. You can't wait for them to arrive, the objects of your love, the children with their ruddy exhilaration, the wife weary of the traffic, how she thought she'd never make it back. The click of the antilock brakes as the tires skid slightly on the ice, the burp of the handbrake before she shuts the engine off and trudges up the steps inside. No, no, my friend, this movie can't go on. We can't insist on it, and pretend to live by it. The rest of the world knows too much about us now.

/ /

Sometimes at night a car
playing a loud stereo rolls

down the street as if on patrol.
It may not be the same car,
but I always think it is.

The sounds the car releases
hover like a large,
awkward shadow
darkening lawns, turning
the white houses gray.

There were nights
I stayed up waiting for it,
excited behind a window

or even under the murky
lights of the street.

I too want to possess
that kind of dread. I want
to be ready when the impulse
that brings the car here
grows wings and beaks.

/ /

Let's try again. Human character and the nature of the polis,
arranged, established. Plato, not Montesquieu, not yet.

How to see it when you're not in it, or don't think you're in it? I
mean at this very moment, where are they, your fellow citizens?

They're living their lives.

You talk about them as if they're a different species.

It's not that they're different. It's not even their need to normalize
their difference. It's that they're trying to paint the whole world the
color they want to see. They're actively doing that, trying to bring on
the second coming. It's a long history of projection. Think of
Kinsey.

Are you arguing it's the failure of the Enlightenment project again?

That too. Think of China; half of the middle class are using whitening
creams, the poor ones using mercury. Think of Michael Jackson's
skin.

/ /

Things oscillate within things,
the brain feeding on itself and growing.

//

The party's general secretary ran out of the villa shooting, a Land Cruiser waiting over the fence. They got him in the end. Three packs of Rothman International and a bottle of Aramis in his briefcase.

Did you send him the Rothmans?

No, the Aramis. One of the lab people said he put something in it that would make him hallucinate or cause severe depression. I can't remember which.

Also through the Kuwaiti ambassador?

Yeah, he was a helpful little fellow. That short, and God knows how many wives he had.

Did it work, the Aramis?

Not exactly. We convinced the Saudis to cancel their aid package, and that caused severe economic depression.

That'll do.

You bet.

//

And what about him? He's no Yoo, he's not like her. He's on your side, don't you think?

First you noticed how he got blamed for charisma. So they don't have charisma, and they'll begin to say it's like dancing or basketball. We're not good at it, you can have it. We're the people that make the trains run on time. Then they'll say you have no substance, you're just a dance and song. Or your substance is the wrong stuff, you're not

tough enough or you're too dangerous. It becomes a way of calling
you monkey and wimp and Hitler all at the same time.

/ /

It is for this reason that I have killed the child;
it is for this reason that I have poked a hole in the ship;
that I have rebuilt the wall.

Imagine not asking the questions.
That's the trust you must begin to afford.

/ /

If you talk to the Chinese about cheap labor, they begin to complain
about Vietnamese competitiveness.

And who are the Vietnamese complaining about?

Bangladesh. And the Bengladeshis are really pissed at the Burmese.

/ /

"Such a government does not break men's will, but softens, bends,
and guides it; it seldom enjoins, but often inhibits action; it does not
destroy anything, but prevents much from being born; it is not at all
tyrannical but it hinders, restrains, enervates, stifles, and stultifies."

/ /

On the same day I heard the story of the man who killed his child we,
I mean I, saw a man wearing a vapor mask, the cheap kind you find
at a hardware store. He looked exhausted, his arms slumped. It was

about eleven at night, the street filled with young people bar-hopping and dressed in fashionable clothes. In the seconds it took us to pass him sitting in front of an empty coffee shop, I could see that there was a hole below the mask, no bridge of a nose, only a hole about two inches wide. I asked her if she saw anything, and she said, "What?" and so I said nothing, while inside me everything went down as if falling into a giant drain.

/ /

Dear B:

To say all the new thinking resembles all the old thinking is to say the fork in the road where one stood indecisive was not a crossroad at all, because one has not moved. Rather it's the earth that has lurched under us like a moving sidewalk in an airport, some passengers standing, others rushing past, the bleep-bleep of the golf carts joyriding the elderly to one of their final destinations. Or when the airliner or the train next to yours moves and you think you've moved. This is not to say that it is only a matter of perception, but that the classics do not console enough. Or maybe that they console too much. You talk about Brutus's purple mantle, and Anthony's decision to behead the poor soul who stole it. If you don't think it's about consolation then why revert back to that code? And Horace's farm, a gift from a patron who loved his poetry, or merely loved the idea of befriending a poet and patronizing him. You'd only have to watch TV to see traces of that, "the artist" surrounded by his entourage, the affluence factor a tax deduction, the drugs an entertainment expense, a hedge fund exec with a salary (payment made in salt) of five hundred million dollars, the acreage outside his mansion the size of modern day Carthage. You only have to see the present to realize how false the past can be. Again, Horace's farm, his free-range cows feeding on acorns. Acorns! and the spring of cold healing water. Let's just admit that the spring was mere superstition, or nostalgia steeped in superstition, and the cows an easy romanticism. But what of the air that feeds the thinking? This country will consume forty five million metric tons of beef, thirty two million of pork. Maybe you're thinking of Ulysses now, doing a cameo as a swineherd a few miles downwind from you where the levels of sulfur in the nearby springs are three thousand times what is humanly tolerable. To wish upon dying a happy man having lived in virtue and having died, if need be, holding fast to, or because of holding fast, to one's conviction . . . Virtue, (antonym: vice, impurity). Something in me says "Fortune" instead, which is another way of saying "Fat Chance," which is to say, each particular just about erases the luminous clarity of a general ideal.

/ /

Where are they? I mean when do you meet them, really, these fellow citizens?

On airplanes mainly. They are perfect research subjects then. So oblivious, they'd be reading golf magazines, spread sheets, or spy novels or romances or watching video, fully absorbed. It's fascinating, the quiet, the solitude.

Does it bother you that you just observe?

It's better than being oblivious.

How do you belong when you just observe?

You make observation your home.

/ /

I am 18, married with 3 children. I spend all day smashing the foundations of the wall around what was the United States embassy to retrieve the steel rods used to reinforce the concrete. I get about 30 rods a day but I have to give half of them to the gunman who

controls the area I work. He doesn't control the whole US embassy—
just the wall. The embassy grounds have been divided up between
about 20 gunmen and people are working for them all. I have been
doing this for about 3 years and have gone 3 km around the wall. I
sell the rods to people building new houses.

/ /

Simply sucked him, something inside of that screen just vacuumed
him.

What to call where he ended up then? What word best fits where he
ended up?

A treatment plant, maybe. An incinerator. Something that just turns
you into some kind of sludge.

Does it help to think of him in this way?

No, it doesn't. I feel like I'm holding that disgusting stuff in my hands,
and sometimes it feels like it's inside me, like I'm scooping it out of
myself.

Why does it feel like that, you think?

Because I think I loved him, but really I was physically repulsed by
him. Maybe I detected all along that he'd turn out horrible, that he's
horrible inside. But sometimes I feel it's just guilt, that I should have
loved him, or allowed him to love me, and then all of this would not
have happened. I mean he was great, or in some ways, is still a great,
sensitive guy. It wasn't like some façade had been lifted and suddenly
he showed his real face. There's no way for you to see that ugliness.
Until now, you, or I can't see it. But I know it's there.

/ /

The wonder of it she'd sung,
the wonder she'd sprung into the world singing,

and you say bless this goodness
wrung of amnesia, of the whips' hieroglyphs,

this song rattling the creaking church,
this gale of cool air washing away the savannah's moss.

Hearth in winter, Abel's
blood streaming endless from your veins.

/ /

Long ago plantation slaves developed a code so the master doesn't understand. I've heard also about some masters who developed a code so the slaves don't understand. Now it's the master's poor offspring talking in code. They'll look you in the eye and give you a civil answer. And what they mean by looking you in the eye is that it's all about race, that nothing has changed.

/ /

Since I killed my child I have died ten times and each time have returned a lesser being. Right now, I feel that a rat or a pig is an honorable being compared to me. Even a maggot. I am afraid I will go on dying like this and returning. I do not want to know the end of this process. I already know what God can do to a man. And I know that in God's parables there are signs for those who think and deliberate. I am one of the stories now, one of the signs.

/ /

Any way, in my line of work, it's best that an outsider tells you what it's like, or tells you what you are. That's what Joseph Brodsky said.

Please don't quote that ass kisser to me.

Don't you want to know what kind of outsider you can be?

I told you we were just in Hawaii. In Maui as we drove around, we saw many rental cars of the same model we rented. Couples dressed like us driving around the whole island trying to finish it in one day. And I realized I was one of them.

/ /

Oh, it was a big party, rented the country club ballroom, the dad clowning, tied his necktie around his forehead. I asked the band leader to play something and she said "sure" and I waited a long time, but she didn't play my song. No, not, "A change gonna come." Those people wouldn't know what to do if you played that to them. Oh, she sang it alright, and she did a great job, then she came up to me and said, "Sucker where's my money?" I didn't give her any money. It just didn't feel right then. Any way later that night I fucked her, but she made so much noise I had to stop.

/ /

I am 22 years old. I drive this bus on a 30 km route. On the way, we go through 6 checkpoints run by different militias. I pay a fee to all of them and show them respect. We have a saying, "The man who becomes your mother's husband becomes your uncle."

/ /

You start with an elementary education system. You let the Mormons or evangelicals do that. In English, if you can. At any rate, once you

have literacy, English will come along. That's your labor source right
there. Then the Indians or Chinese or Brazilians can start a factory
and get a concession on the mineral or oil resources. Our guys will
sell the equipment, and get in on the action once more money is to be
made. There's got to be a TV station with Mexican or Venezuelan or
Turkish soap operas so people will know what to buy once they have
money. Then you find a local leader who needs weapons and you arm
him for a while, and later set him up in some drug trade to self-
finance. And he keeps everybody in line for you. That's it in a
nutshell.

/ /

You want to know the parameters of public life, and you realize the
extent of it when public opinion is leaning towards ending the war.

When enough of them are killed, they'll reach for it. When they
can't describe their dead as heroes anymore, they'll reach for it.

That's why the Vietnam memorial is as short as it is. How long
would it go on, if it had all the names of the people killed in that
war.

Forget it. Those people are so gone you can't even think of them as
people anymore.

They are leaves of grass.

The handkerchief of the Lord,
a scented gift and remembrancer designedly dropt,
bearing the owner's name . . .

You're right, they're nothing to us now.

Never were.

/ /

You've got to admit that we're all white people now. Everybody that got killed in that war is White, all got killed for Whitie. Even the people in China are White people now. That's what a lot of these brown or yellow conservatives are really saying, and even they don't realize what they're getting at. They're saying race doesn't matter because they've become White.

/ /

He'd play a long tune, so that he'd go out and smoke. Yeah, he did have that pimp talk that all DJ's have, a voice that got under your skin when you're vulnerable, and behind the microphone he spoke to that vulnerability, one on one. I mean it was medicinal, a kind of easy spirituality. Sometimes he read from a book or a magazine, made it seem the studio was a happening place, and all sorts of people showed up at his door. You'd turn on the radio and he'd be there talking, and you'd just drive and he'd play something long, "Green Sleeves" say, and you'd go out and smoke a joint together. Even the campus cops knew what was going on, and they didn't mind because they thought, if it wasn't harmless, what he was doing was at least cool. I just want to remember that, only that about him, the fact that anybody lonely with a joint knew where to go.

/ /

You think it can be fixed?

It's already fixed when all the factions want to be on your side. They'll want you to provide them advisors and sell them arms. And when they get tired, that's when they need another set of advisors and contractors and suppliers and so on. Just keep your casualties down and none will be worse for the wear.

Who is talking now? Which "we" are you inserting yourself into now?

In the car, she'd received a phone call just as the story of the pounded child began on the radio. And when I heard the father tell how he killed his child, I cried out in disbelief. She turned to me, and later asked what made me cry out, and I wanted to say that it was the story on the radio, but instead said, "it's something I forgot to do." That's what I told her. Of course, I want to protect her, I don't know if there's anything else I can do, or I feel I can do, or even if what I feel for her will allow me to do anything else but that. If noting else, I'll protect her, I keep telling myself.

Is that a good feeling, your desire to protect her?

It is.

You think you can build on it.

It's all I got now.

/ /

Dear A:
You ask for the fissure
that lets the air in, or the fumes out.
I'm sorry, but there's none.

/ /

The other scenario is that he'll win and they'll cripple him within a year. You'll be surprised by the variety of people who'll go after him. He's already compromised a lot to get the bankers and the drug companies to finance him and he's moved away from the vision that made him seem like a transformative figure. Wait until those who supported him feel betrayed, and see how those sitting on the sidelines rush in like hyenas after the kill.

/ /

Back then you knew the guys who worked for the agency easily
They were the ones who could not speak the local language, didn't even try.

Now they have computers doing that. You tap the phone lines of the target and you plug the voice transmission into the software and you get instant translation. But guess who's doing the compulinguistics?

Certainly not people like you and me.

It's called the karma of yellow/brown folks.

/ /

If it irks the heart.
If it befits the many, and the one.
If it restores the bones' logarithm.
If it goes on dissolving.
If the one can live its double.
If it brings the narcissus from underwater
to join his twin.

/ /

A dream between us
fogging what we want to see . . .
A prison, but then everywhere else is a prison . . .
Who aint a slave, asks Ishmael.
The worse form of government except for all the others, etc . . .
To wipe the glass window with a muddy rag,
enclosing us within the house upon the Malibu hills.
What girds one's bearing against attention?
What will send the nerves to their first apprehensions?
A picture now.
A tremble.
A night full of furor.

/ /

I know that night is like that, that it allows for boundaries to oscillate. You know it when you step on your lawn shoeless at night with dew cold at first on your feet, a coldness that begins to feel normal after a while. Night works on itself, works worlds, owns a law, and him smoking outside the station is like seeing a raccoon with pups crossing a road to hide out in a drain hole. Night is like that, and he lived it. But a raccoon wouldn't do what he did, and then he takes pictures of it and distribute them to the rest of the perverted world. You can't call it a mistake, or some human error, and after all of that, there's no one to blame here, not even him. And I can't say it's ideology, capitalism, materialism, or any kind of social psychology. It's some kind of night that sucks you into it, that dazzles you and would not let go of you. And you think you're in it alone, and you're free being all alone, and then you realize the night is crowded and full of people groping for anything they can reach. Anything.

/ /

Chevron used to have a ship named after her.

Was that before or after she got into government?

Before. They changed the name once she got into government. It would have been too much. The appearance of conflict of interest, you know.

Did she ever work for them?

Not exactly. But you could say she worked for the cause.

/ /

I want to give you a rose.
I have to make it.
That's how pure my gift must be.

/ /

And these idiots still think we lost Vietnam.

On My Mind

It was enough to see her gold tooth
her recline in the fold-up chair,
the satisfaction, a menthol cigarette—
bought them by the carton now.

June in Chattanooga, seventh day
in the factory and she was—
a few words to explain   what she was—

sold that clunker years ago
a Nissan, a boyfriend
on the pill   everything's low fat.

She talked, the way I'd seen
other women talk, so much
laughter, can't count on it healing,

yet a wiliness for keeping
a man around   the boy in school
the daughter unpregnant.

The more I looked upon her
the more I loved her,
but not for too long

for she could brush me away
like a curl of smoke.
I looked upon her nonetheless,

how each moment
was stolen back
from a life she'd started long ago.

I was slapping goo
on thick socks called Toestees.
It was still hot at midnight
when I punched in my time card
for the last time.

I think her name was Georgia.

Trees

For Nadia Benabid

Sad like a bird caught in the spill,
                    the beach covered in patches,
tubercular.

In the cold air, oil hardens gloved fists around the birds' throats.

Sad, the stages skipped, the speed of the inevitable.

What to testify for? or against? Who to listen and judge?

Perhaps it's enough to speak of trees.

                    / /

To live under this maple

—"Greedy tree," neighbor says, "sucks all the water out—

to touch its thirst, to assure it— Be fair.

To see you, a shadow tangled among its roots,
released into the air—to whisper into its ears,
or to slip a message under its wings.

Heart locked out of its chambers.
Heart, a branch cut from a tree.

                    / /

Letter from a friend—

"geese, leaves, speeding clouds. Need I say more?"

Friend, please, say more.

//

I've seen the faces, razed hamlets, injured streets.
Read the eyes dragging centuries of lead.

The body rises to its solemn habits.

I have seen it transfigured, martyred seeking murder.
Seen it hung from a tree.

//

By the seashore, palms and sun, clouds sailing inland.
Time to get lost.

This palm is my anchor, I begin to think.

By the shore, tropical fruit, scents lingering in resinous air.
I think I understand, I begin to think.

Last night, a bright road stretched on,
a thread fallen from a storm cloud.

There was so much noise and shivering,
hard to believe anything slept in the sugarcane fields.

//

If only to see it grow from seed to leaf.
The word, the words, the tree of mind.

If one can prune it or graft a bough from another.
If one can cut it and hammer it or tighten its screws.

If one can uproot it, live the darkness it lives.

Tocqueville

Khaled Mattawa

To look inside, count years . . .

Word, cell, germ, electron.
Leaves, lemon, cinnamon, plum, red delicious.

O man bagging them,
O woman driving the truck picking them up.

/ /

Decided—clear out the buckthorns—"invasive species"—planted
    stunted pines.

Decided—pull out bushes, build a stone fence.

Decided—take down maple, enlarge the garage.

All the secret keepers are dead.

/ /

Her New Jersey apartment a piece of Paris
with a view of the Luxemburg.
Thick bread and wine, fancy bottled water,
books floor to ceiling, the soundtrack 50s jazz,
ashtrays emptied refilled, cigarettes,
exotic brands sampled like chocolates,
and chocolates, orgasms of liqueur.

The trees rose taller than her balcony.
We didn't know they were laughing.
Never knew their names.

//

Surprised the eucalyptus trees still there.
Somewhere else they would've have been burned for fuel.

Still shaggy, dusty like a poor man's flock
of bickering hens.

The world tread past them a hundred years,
the stream of cars thicker,
parades, executions, wedding cavalcades.

For all I'd been through—my long wait, this return,
and their unchanged state—

a bad omen, say the doubtful bones.

//

A road leading to the sea, a small road like a child
walking a forest before it learned how to fear.

Trees silent, wind withdrawn.

A small road, out of the sea, made by those
who could no longer swim with their terrors.

//

Why do they nod to me like dogs
lifting, lowering heads wanting to play?

Should I give them words that sprout
from the mouths of this land
or the language in my bones?

Should I group them by touch or color—
trees of pearly, gray smooth bark,
of leaves like old women's hands,
trees of round, dark red fruit?

Should I name them to their stories—
tree that hides the stop sign in summer,
tree where I once shot a bird,
tree I planted to cast a shadow on her grave?

Power Point III

(December 2006-February 2007)

A droning, the pulseless siphoning sound of jet engines
    flying over the Atlantic ocean.

> Context/Daydream

Someone enters the bathroom and locks the door.
She or he (most likely a he)
notices that bathrooms on commercial airliners
are all the same, regardless of "class."

At that very moment he or she is the sugar and protein molecules
feeding the brain of his nation/culture, but does not know it.

> CHORUS: Don't worry, dear reader, he is not you

Perhaps it's the recycled air, he thinks
(more oxygen here than for the folks down in economy)

and yes it's horrifying the vision he has: the plane suddenly crashing,
out of the blue, into the blue.

Political consequences aside, official investigations and adjustments
of Boeing/Airbus stock aside

his mind races, is racing toward:

What will they say?

        / /

To know to live to justify	to live to know
to justify to live	
for the dog lapping water	in an ancient parable
for him who sought protection	with blood on his hands
for the thoughtful fox leaping	like a harpoon into snow
for him who has stopped	finding his heart

Tocqueville

Khaled Mattawa

for the mouse caught in jaws   the one housed in a cage
for him of the reeking breath   belly full of human flesh
            to know to justify to live
            further the further to know

Context/Daydream

/ /

       But what to make of:

Found in Naples
lying on his face,
he's ranted so often
his silence too was a rant.

In that final lying down,
what thought did he bury
in the dingy marble
of the rented flat?

Grief Matrix	Case 1	Case 2	Case 3	Case 4
Symbolism	has implants that looked like another ass on her chest	the kind of guy who would fight for a losing cause	you say Stalin, I say Saladin	gospel + brothel = jail as homage to slavery
Pataphysics	I profess myself an enemy to all other joys (marries octogenarian for love)	pardons "I'm not a (Crook) Coriolanus"	for I have erected a dam against flowing water	notice the motion of the feet
Origin	the one whom the circle was made for (context D. W. Griffith)	moderation to the point of indecency	murder ad nauseam in cahoots with national aspirations	—*please please please* as sucker punch
Form	notice the motions of the mouth (I cannot heave my love in my mouth)	when there's no destination, that's too far	wide gash on throat upon surrender of body	for I am the nose of the Lord of breath
Petit Histoire	When she was dear to us, we did hold her so;/But now her price is fall'n	stepfather a magnificent person, mother equally wonderful. Couldn't have written better prescription for	Halabjah	I keep slip-ping slip-ping slip-ping

You return to the hotel room and she's cleaning it. You don't know
        what to do
and she doesn't know what to do either.

You glance at her hips, at their fullness. She takes you in too.

What would happen if you gently held her wrist and closed the
        door?

You do not speak her language,
you do not want to speak her language when you undo her hair pin,
and run fingers from the base of her neck into her biblical fleece.

You think about the consequences of the blonde highlights in her hair.

You think how much you and she will give to this moment,
how to keep it from spilling into an abyss.

It must remain beyond words,

that scent of soap and sweat wafting from the lavender concaves
        below her arms, and the distance
it takes for your cheeks to caress her breasts.

Once you are inside her, and as she swivels you into the angles of her
        pleasure,
you feel justified and transcendent.

Then you're the shy one when it's over.

> Context/Daydream

She has work still, and a supervisor to explain her delay to.

Of course, she'll take the hard currency.

You want to see her another time, but you never see her again.

/ /

CUT TO:
(home movie taken by phone camera)

"If he's gonna be buried, I'monna jump and be buried with him,"
she says.

"Think of the girl you'd just given life to," nothing else they could
tell her.

Was it later or before that she posed lying down with the judge that
granted her citizenship?

Guilt/remorse/circumspection

like drops of water on wax paper, unabsorbable.

She took off her shoes as she prepared to jump into her son's grave.
Can you imagine that?

Why did she take them off?

Because they're expensive.

Consolation Matrix	Case 1	Case 2	Case 3	Case 4
Dispersal	Gods, gods! 'tis strange that from their cold'st neglect/ My love should kindle such inflamed respect	appeases Cyclop (Poles do not consider themselves dominated by CCCP)	demon/bear in the woods (Enkidu as Cyclop)	into the fuuuuuuuuture
Centering	Lawsuit against NY magazine; against step-son (?) for inheritance; to declare bankruptcy; to determine paternity of daughter	for I have not extinguished a fire in its critical moment	for I have caused pain and weeping	among first inductees into Rock and Roll Hall of Fame
Semantics	most rich, being poor;/ Most choice, forsaken; and most loved, despised!	for I have not killed	for I have killed, for I have commanded to kill	caliban as Enkidu followed by Mick Jagger as Ferdinand to save Miranda
Symptom	for I do not know that which should not be	for I have not added weight to the balance	Rathe to destroy, niggard in charity	for I have made labors in excess of what should be done for me

CUT TO (interior/nighttime: sweeping shot of scraps of
paper on kitchen table, steam rising from a
boiling pot, half drunk bottle of red wine,
scratchy foreign music on the stereo, someone
is washing dishes and trying to assemble an
eulogy for a memorial service)

Audio clip: *Blessings to you, date palm shading the yard . . .*

Paper scrap 1:   In Anchorage, what lead you there, aristocrat of
democracy?

Photo: of deceased wearing sunglasses facing TV screen
with static

Audio clip: *dangling braids over the ones I love*

Paper scrap 2:   the fustiness, the ancient beard,
the house made from sun-baked bricks,
its salted sheepskins,
the breath of dried palm fronds.

Audio clip: *Are these rags or sails I see?*

Paper scrap 3:   The Newfoundland sea so cold,
a rake tearing the light into shreds

Audio clip: *a boat has gone and left me . . .*

Paper scrap 4:   A nest buoyed by the wind,
grass growing on the tip of a great fire

/ /

CUT TO
(short film/allegory/organization chart)
(triple-split screen)

three cool customers

President of U.S.	Vice President of U.S.	U.S. Secretary of Defense

preparing to leave a

stock market/casino	fundraiser/casino	senate hearing/casino

the chips they are cashing in
are shrunken human skulls

the cashier is

CHORUS: It could be you, dear reader

It's happy hour

three chipper waitresses

U.S. Secretary of State	Under Secretary of Public Diplomacy and Public Affairs	Director of National Endowment for Democracy

serving new drinks

Al-Hurra	Blackwater	IED

Tagline:

Ever-returning spring,	trinity sure to me	you bring

/ /

You've thought about it, and allowed your thoughts to stray from their kindling:

You fucked, you helped her, you made love. He's a reactionary, he's a visionary, he was once ahead of his time, but is now behind it; he was clear-eyed; he was a cantankerous romantic. You used her. Everyone used him. He is dead and she is alive, why does the image of one bring up the image of the other?

And you begin to think the "world,"

Context/Daydream

       if such a word means anything,

is made up of such secrets for the world to be the world.

What brought you to her city in the first place, for where else could such confidences be made and thrown into a well?

Reverence Matrix	Case 1	Case 2	Case 3	Case 4
Distance	buried next to son in Lakeview Memorial Gardens and Mausoleum (both dead from overdosing on prescription drugs)	dies in California, shown in state in Washington D.C., buried in hometown (pilot insists deceased gets last look)	buried 45 miles from birthplace)	lost in the wilderness, lost in the bitterness
Participation	5 men claimed parentage of daughter	the green casque has outdone your elegance	led failed assassination attempt on country's president	the acrobatics of keeping the fire, the agility to take down Cyclop in the woods
Creation	playmate of the year, 1992	you twain/ Rule in this realm, and the gored state sustain	classical music audience in Tel Aviv dressed in gas masks	Thou didst prevent me; I had peopled else/ This isle with Calibans
Rhetoric	Like my body?	We cannot miss him: he does make our fire,/ Fetch in our wood and serves in offices/ That profit us	Leads 9th largest army in the world. Exeunt: I took by the throat the circumcised dog,/ And smote him, thus	There's wood enough within
Synthesis	someone with habits not allowed our subjects wins, not the record producer, or concert promoter, not arms	dealer or torturer, or pharmaceutics pusher wins, someone who has the consumer/ voter on a leash, defined not thru	hubris, but demography, someone who trades in abstractions, whose tongue is tapping	the spine of the culture, who holds on to them to feel what it's like to hold the culture by its Mirandas

And what took him to Naples? Newfoundland, Texas, Alaska?

To know to live to justify to live to know to justify to live

the verbs like dolphins leaping over one another

and so goes the plan against the unbearable will to break down and
sing:

and to live to justify to know is

to have a secret, to mourn what no one but you can mourn.

                        / /

                Where do you absent yourself/
                once danger or triumph pass/

                Where are you,/
                for whom I have found no names/

                My bones know you/
                the way the stars know you/

                A dumb reckoning/
                like air lost in air/

                like prey disappearing/
                into the camouflage of the herd/

You who are everything/
essence and breed/

Where are you/
when my life belongs to me/

and I am free/
of it/

Come to me/
and be my silence/

Redemption Matrix	Case 1	Case 2	Case 3	Case 4
Play	"You sure you don't like my body?"	semi-pro (turned down offers from Detroit Lions and Green Bay Packers)	for I have cut off electricity on households that refused to join literacy program	a longing
Design	understands the national grid, vaginal mouth on TV, medium is money, message to penis/soul	"didn't think voters would like him marrying a divorced ex-dancer"	Enkidu + Cyclop = Caliban	to have gathered from the air a live tradition
Change	the moment is only itself, but it's intense and so it feels like a long time	"Funky President (People It's Bad)"	N/A	from a fine old eye, the unconquered (famous) Flame(s)
Hierarchy	she's trash, but you can't have her	he knows the circle is broken and needs welding, needs fire	first-round pick in post-Soviet draft	most sampled in the world
Process	subject, mother, father divorces 4 times respectively	want democracy + don't want freedom = domestic spying + Guantanamo	want freedom + don't want democracy = dictatorship + civil war	make them tired; that's what they came for

Nice try to explain what happened in that hotel room, in the middle
of the day, no less.

But yes, go ahead think of elegy as the devil's last kernel of regret,
a thin stream that has run as long as speech runs
as long as tears fall from human eyes
as long as eyes are plucked from human skulls.

<table>
<tr><td>Context/Daydream</td></tr>
</table>

Think of it as the gap between a past thought reasonable in its time
    that is no longer conceivable

and whatever is eternal is now
convertible to exchange like a time-order
waiting to pounce on appropriate value

something believed finite, but vast deposits of it continue to be found
                (That's where the massacres take place)

to help us know to live to justify to live to know to justify to live
the tide and its endless takings

the moment that words interfere and divvy the limbs' motions

and divvy the limbs.

Transfiguration Index	Case 1	Case 2	Case 3	Case 4
Mystery/Logo	Trimspa	number retired at alma mater	rapist/raped dialectic with population	I/you feel good
Process	It's a man's man's world	all in the diffidence that faltered	beaten by step-father, offered agricultural loans by U.S. for war on neighbor	an icon you can sample your 'larger' culture through
Closure	in reference to white female, she's not breathing	a ripening afterwards by a nation hankering for decency	"Is this what you call manhood?"	the power to sample is the source of subjectivity and national character
Metaphysics	if it helps her, what wonders would it do for you	Rodin's thinker with an erection (Fanon)	imagine the devil hired on retainer	Imagine his glove compartment chockful of amphetamines

First snow, first week of December

you're out smoking (never inside since the baby'd come).

The cars pass slow and wobbly
each with only the driver inside.

Where are you going and coming from
my townspeople, comrades?

4.5 million dead in the Congo—the number slightly less or more—

the pile of them in the forest being burned, King Leopold as eternal
    kindling

> CHORUS: Better run along now, dear reader, and
>   seek out your own redemption

the other piles, the other kindling.

My townspeople, my comrades
going and coming from,

smoking outside since the baby'd come.

Elegy, a product consumed by a man alone in a hotel room exists in
the grid of one, and in the grid of nine billion. To the man alone, a
comfort:

each burning   his share   of the trees

Before

Somewhere beyond faith and grace there is
the footprint of logic lost in the purest light.

Not hidden at all, but a vehicle, a necessity, neither
mop nor bucket, but whatever gives the floor its shine.

The sun through the window pours on the floor,
and the wood glistens as if in praise.
As if a child breaking into a run. That is what I see

through the window now. A child breaking
into a run for the simple flame that must burn
and because there are such words.

Of course, I could be wailing.
Of course, the child is not a memory,
only a gesture on my part.

Yesterday, I fed a friend's cat and talked to her,
the town was emptied and filled with
snow embroidered with tire tracks.

I fed a friend's cat and she rubbed her sides against my calves.

The thing to say now is that I am in the middle of a life
in a house with the owners on holiday.

Or to say a car engine hums (the owner forgetting
the keys inside), and is on its way to a crystalline loss.

Here deduction is howling at an oncoming storm.

The thing is, I fed a friend's cat and later poured
a bowl of milk for her and she sniffed it,
barely licked it, and left.

The thought is. The life is.

I've visited graves—tombstones ten feet high.
I ran through the cemetery and laughed my Cairo laugh.
I wanted to be arrested by the police, wanted

someone to take down what I had to say.
Whatever I would have said then would have been the truth.

But there was no one there.
Only dust and a shitload of romance.

Only dust and the hum of the interstate. Detroit,
Toledo, the hitchhiker hums a foreign song.

I feed the cat and talk to her.
I take the milk away and begin to forget
and the cat stares at the missing bowl.

Billions of snowflakes in between,
and the befores that follow the first before.

Notes

"On the Difficulty of Documentation" is written in response to the photographs of Myrtle Winter. A selection of Winter's photographs appear in *I Would Have Smiled: Photographing the Palestinian Refugee Experience,* published by the Institute for Palestine Studies, 2009. The poems excerpted are Thomas Wyatt's "They flee from me Sometime did me Seek" and Bertolt Brecht's "To Posterity," translated by T. R. Hays.

"Power Point I" draws on the articles in an issue of *The New Yorker,* February 3, 2003.

Power Point II" borrows from William Carlos Williams's "To a Poor Old Woman."

"Terrorist" draws on analyses by Khalid Sohail, Avishai Margalit, and Mia Bloom.

"Tocqueville" alludes to and excerpts from David Bethea's *Joseph Brodsky and the Creation of Exile*; Vijay Prashad's *The Karma of Brown Folk*; *Habits of the Heart: Individualism and Commitment in American Life,* by Robert Bellah et al; Frantz Fanon's *Black Skin, White Masks* and *Wretched of the Earth*; Tocqueville's *Democracy in America* (the George Lawrence translation); Edward Said's *Reflections on Exile*; The Quran 18: 65-82; Homi Bhabha's *The Location of Culture*; Robert Hass' "Meditation at Lagunitas"; Robert Pinsky's *An Explanation of America*; Derek Walcott's "Guyana"; Walt Whitman's "Song of Myself." The poem paraphrases several stories from"Life in Somalia: Mahamut's Story," (http://news.bbc.co.uk/2/hi/africa/4040889.stm). The individuals whose stories are re-told here are: Mahamut Issa Abdi, Abdidir Ali Hashi, Muktar 'Idi' Ramadan, Abdi Dahir Guled. The poem also retells the story of musician Mohamed Bangura based on "The Refugee All-Stars of Sierra Leone Country," (http://www.pri.or/theworld/?q=node/2027). The phrase, "God knows how many wives he had" is a paraphrase of a comment made by George Bernard Shaw regarding Rabindranath Tagore (Krishna Dutta and Andrew Robinson's, *Rabindranath Tagore: A Myriad Minded Man,* 1997).

"On My Mind" borrows two lines from Whitman's "The Sleepers."

"Trees" borrows the phrase "swim with terror" from Adrienne Rich's poem "Two Movements" in *Dark Fields of the Republic.*

"Power Point III" incorporates a few phrases from George W. S. Trow's *The Context of No Context.* And from Whitman's "When Lilacs Last in the Door-yard Bloom'd." I'm indebted to David Baker's essay, "Elegy and Eros: Configuring Grief" (published in *Radiant Lyric: Essays on Lyric Poetry,* 2007) for its suggestiveness. The design of the matrices is indebted to the work of Ihab Hassan.

Acknowledgments

I am indebted to Gretchen Knapp, T. J. Anderson III, Philip Metres, and Megan Levad for feedback on this manuscript in various stages of its development.

I wish also to thank Marianne Swierenga and the rest of the staff at New Issues for the patience and hard work on the production of this book.

I am grateful to the editors of the following journals for publishing earlier versions of these poems.

Black Warrior Review: "Bread and Butter"

The Canary: "Power Point I"

The Colorado Review: "Power Point III"

Effing: "Power Point II"

Green Mountains Review: "On the Difficulty of Documentation" and "Trees"

Massachusetts Review: "Before"

Indiana Review: "Later, Later"

Mizna: "Ecclesiastes"

/NOR (New Ohio Review): "Tocqueville"

Visions International: "Airporter"

"Ecclesiastes," appeared in the *Pushcart Prize Anthology XXVIII*, 2004. "Power Point I" appeared in the *Pushcart Prize Anthology XXXI*, 2007. "Terrorist" appeared in *We Begin Here: Poems for Palestine and Lebanon*, Kamal Boullata and Kathy Engel, editors, Interlink Books, 2007.

photo by Amanda Abel

Khaled Mattawa was born in Benghazi, Libya in 1964 and immigrated to the U.S. in his teens. He is the author of three previous books of poetry, *Ismailia Eclipse* (Sheep Meadow, 1995), *Zodiac of Echoes* (Ausable, 2003), and *Amorisco* (Ausable, 2008). Mattawa has translated eight volumes of contemporary Arabic poetry and co-edited two anthologies of Arab American literature. He has received a Guggenheim fellowship, an NEA translation grant, the Alfred Hodder Fellowship from Princeton University, the PEN American Center Poetry Translation Prize, and three Pushcart Prizes. Mattawa teaches in the MFA (Creative Writing) Program at the University of Michigan, Ann Arbor.

New Issues Poetry